Wealthy Lotus

You're amazing

just the

way you

are.

www.ingramcontent.com/pod-product-compliance
Lightning Source LLC
Chambersburg PA
CBHW081730220526
45468CB00008B/2044
* 9 7 8 1 7 2 3 8 8 2 1 4 2 *